RUBANK
Ensemble Time

Flexible Instrumentation
TRIOS and QUARTETS

Bb CLARINET
Bb Bass Clarinet

by Harvey Whistler
and Herman Hummel

CONTENTS

AVAILABLE FOR:

Flute (1st, 2nd, 3rd, 4th)	HL04474640
Oboe (3rd)	HL04474640
Bassoon (4th)	HL04474690
Bb Clarinet (1st, 2nd, 3rd, 4th)	HL04474650
Alto Clarinet (3rd)	HL04474660
Bass Clarinet (4th)	HL04474650
Alto Saxophone (1st, 2nd, 3rd, 4th)	HL04474660
Tenor Saxophone (2nd)	HL04474670
Baritone Saxophone (4th)	HL04474660
Bb Trumpet (1st, 2nd, 3rd, 4th)	HL04474670
F Horn (1st, 2nd, 3rd, 4th)	HL04474680
Trombone/Baritone B.C. (1st, 2nd, 3rd, 4th)	HL04474690
Tuba (4th)	HL04474690
Violin (1st, 2nd, 3rd, 4th)	HL04474700
Piano/Conductor	HL04474710

ISBN 978-1-5400-8342-5

RUBANK®

Hal•Leonard®

Visit Hal Leonard Online at
www.halleonard.com

Contact us:
Hal Leonard
7777 West Bluemound Road
Milwaukee, WI 53213
Email: info@halleonard.com

In Europe, contact:
Hal Leonard Europe Limited
42 Wigmore Street
Marylebone, London, W1U 2RN
Email: info@halleonardeurope.com

In Australia, contact:
Hal Leonard Australia Pty. Ltd.
4 Lentara Court
Cheltenham, Victoria, 3192 Australia
Email: info@halleonard.com.au

One and All Rejoice

Chorale

B♭ CLARINET
B♭ Bass Clarinet

RICHARD MASSIE

Copyright MCMXLIII by Rubank, Inc., Chicago, Ill.
International Copyright Secured

2

The Light of All Our Seeing

from the St. John Passion
Chorale

Bb CLARINET
Bb Bass Clarinet

J. S. BACH

3
Concert Waltz
from Oberon

B♭ CLARINET
B♭ Bass Clarinet

C. M. von WEBER

Grazioso

1st

2nd

3rd

4th
(Bass Cl.)

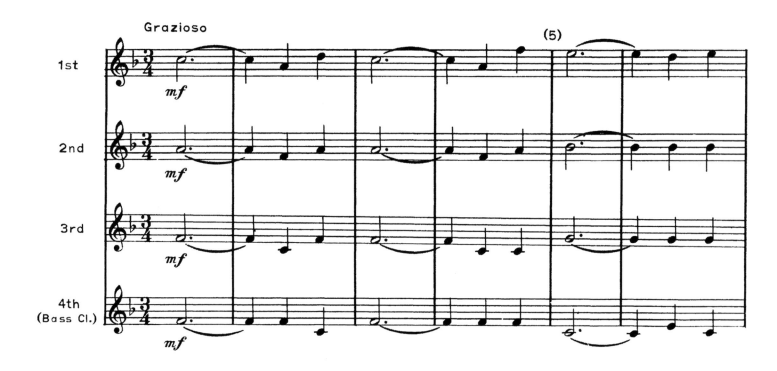

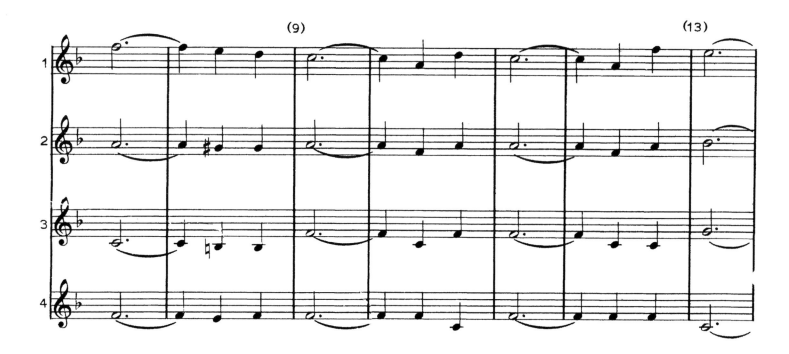

God Rest You Merry, Gentlemen

B♭ CLARINET
B♭ Bass Clarinet

Traditional

5   Integer Vitae

Bb CLARINET
Bb Bass Clarinet

F. FLEMMING

6

Wand'ring One

from The Pirates of Penzance

B♭ CLARINET
B♭ Bass Clarinet

Sir ARTHUR SULLIVAN

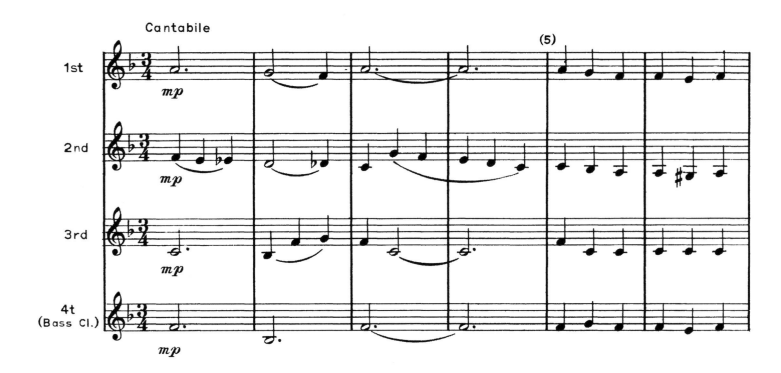

7 The Miller of the Dee

B♭ CLARINET
B♭ Bass Clarinet

Traditional

8

Operatic Air
from IL Trovatore

Bb CLARINET
Bb Bass Clarinet

G. VERDI

9

Vilia Song

from The Merry Widow

B♭ CLARINET
B♭ Bass Clarinet

FRANZ LEHAR

Clarinet/Bass Clarinet

13

10   Blow the Man Down

B♭ CLARINET
B♭ Bass Clarinet

Old Sea Chanty

Lovely is the Evening

11

Bb CLARINET
Bb Bass Clarinet

Traditional

12

The Bell Doth Toll

Traditional

13

The Spring is Come

Dr. HAYES

On Wings of Song

14

B♭ CLARINET
B♭ Bass Clarinet

FELIX MENDELSSOHN

15   Grandfather's Clock

Bb CLARINET
Bb Bass Clarinet

HENRY C. WORK

16

Viennese Melody

B♭ CLARINET
B♭ Bass Clarinet

17 The Parting Hour

Bb CLARINET
Bb Bass Clarinet

FRANZ SCHUBERT

CLARINET SOLOS with Piano Accompaniment

Grade 1

HL04479865	Amazing Grace (incl. opt. duet part) (arr. Walters)
HL04471560	Encore Folio (collection) *Grade 1 to 3*
HL04476839	Nocturne from *Midsummer Night's Dream* (incl. opt duet part) (Mendelssohn/arr. Davis) *Grade 1.5*
HL04479892	Rubank Book of Solos, Easy Level (collection) *Grade 1 to 2*
HL04476811	Sakura, Sakura (incl. opt. duet part) (arr. Walters) *Grade 1.5*

Grade 2

HL04476747	American Patrol (incl. opt. duet part) (Meacham/arr. Hummel)
HL04476758	Chansonette (Barret/arr. Pazemis) *Grade 2.5*
HL04476761	Clarinet Polka (incl. opt. duet and trio parts) (arr. Hummel) *Grade 2.5*
HL04476770	Fantasy-Piece, Op. 73 No. 1 (Schumann/ed. Voxman) *Grade 2.5*
HL04471940	Indispensible Folio (11 Solos with Formative Technique)

BASS CLARINET SOLOS with Piano Accompaniment

HL04476886	Autumn Song (Ostransky) *Grade 3*
HL04476887	The Buffoon (Koepke) *Grade 3*
HL04476782	Jolly Coppersmith (Peters/arr. Jolliff) *Grade 1*
HL04476889	Lamento – Nocturne (Bassi/ed. Voxman) *Grade 4*
HL04476890	Largo and Allegro (Boni/trans. Voxman) *Grade 3*
HL04476892	March of a Marionette (Gounod/arr. Walters) *Grade 2*
HL04476891	Marche Comique (Ostransky) *Grade 3*
HL04476893	Pastorale and Bourrée (German/trans. Voxman) *Grade 4*
HL04476896	Undercurrent – Theme and Variations (Long) *Grade 5*
HL04476897	Vignette (Koepke) *Grade 3*

CLARINET/WOODWIND ENSEMBLES

Instrumentation, grade level as marked

HL04476847	Air and Tarantella (three B♭ w/piano) (Olivadoti) *Grade 2.5*
HL04479518	Andante (from Quartet in D) (four B♭; opt. two B♭, E♭ alto, B♭ bass) (Bohne/arr. Voxman) *Grade 2.5*
HL04479519	Andante and Caprice (four B♭; fourth B♭ bass opt.) (von Gluck/arr. Johnson) *Grade 2.5*
HL04479520	Andante and Minuetto (four B♭) (Bochsa, Schmidt/ed. Voxman) *Grade 2.5*
HL04479521	Aria and Minuet (four B♭; fourth B♭ bass opt.) (Scarlatti/arr. Johnson) *Grade 2*
HL04479522	Bach Chorales for Clarinets (four B♭; fourth B♭ bass opt.) (arr. Johnson) *Grade 1*
HL04474580	Chamber Music for Three Woodwinds, Vol. 1 (flute, oboe or second flute, B♭ clarinet) (ed. Voxman) *Grade 2 to 3*
HL04474590	Chamber Music for Three Woodwinds, Vol. 2 (flute, B♭ clarinet, bassoon) (ed. Voxman) *Grade 2 to 3*
HL04476850	Chanson Triste (three B♭ w/piano) (Dieterich) *Grade 2.5*
HL04479524	Chanson Triste (four B♭; fourth B♭ bass opt.) (Tchaikovsky/arr. Johnson) *Grade 2.5*
HL04479872	The Entertainer (three B♭ w/piano) (Joplin/arr. Walters) *Grade 2.5*
HL04476854	Evensong (three B♭ w/piano) (Koepke) *Grade 2.5*
HL04479526	Galliard and Courante (four B♭; fourth B♭ bass opt.) (Frescobaldi/arr. Johnson) *Grade 2.5*
HL04476728	Prairie Warblers (duet for flute and B♭ clarinet; w/piano) (Endresen) *Grade 2*
HL04479531	Sarabanda and Gavotta (four B♭; fourth B♭ bass opt.) (Corelli/arr. Johnson) *Grade 2.5*
HL04476729	The Two Flyers (duet for flute and B♭ clarinet; w/piano) (Endresen) *Grade 2*